Print & *Cursive* HANDWRITING

WORKBOOK

FOR KIDS & ADULTS

- ✪ Alphabets
- ✪ Practice Sheets
- ✪ Words
- ✪ Coloring

Tara Seals

@2021 COPYRIGHT All rights reserved. The author retains all copyrights in any text, graphic images, and photos in this book. No part of this publication may be reproduced or transmitted in any form or by any means, electronic or mechanical, including photocopying, recording, or any information storage and retrieval system, without permission in writing from the author. This book may be published for educational, business, or sale promotional use. For information, please contact the Special Markets Division.
Send an email to Info@TheBossyEducator.com with your request.

ISBN: 978-0-578-31008-4
Printed in the United States of America
Published by Able Publishing
Illustrated by Raf Has
Editor: L.B. Cadogan

This book belongs to:

_____

Dedication

This Print & Cursive Handwriting Workbook for Kids & Adults is dedicated to the thousands of students I have taught during my amazing journey ranging in ages from 6-78. I know I probably got on your nerves talking about the importance of penmanship, but I am sure you have appreciated my wisdom somewhere along this ride called life. I would also like to dedicate this workbook to my mama. She did not play about my handwriting growing up, and it has truly come in handy more times than I can count. So let's level up, and always remember: Bossy is as bossy does!

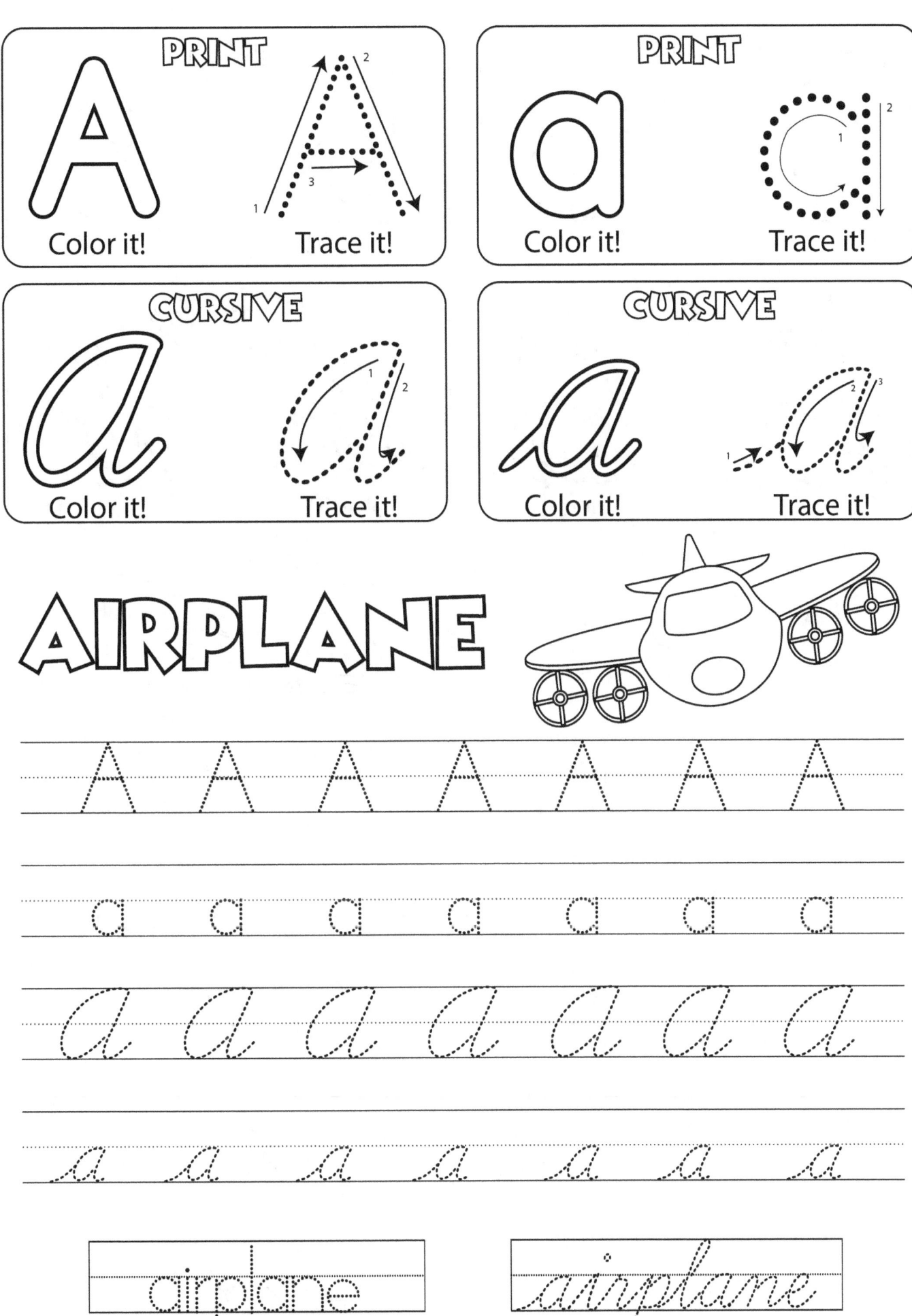

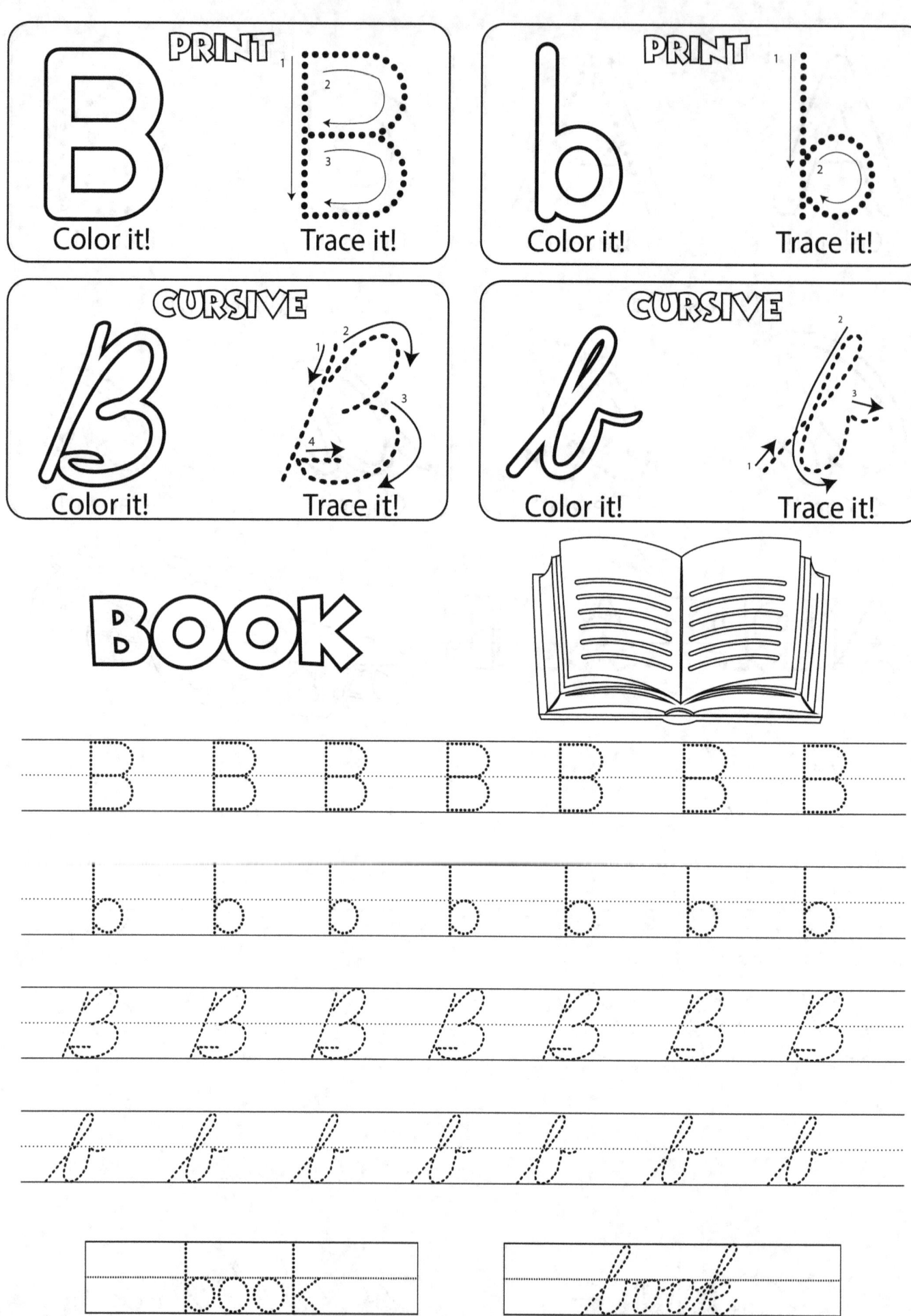

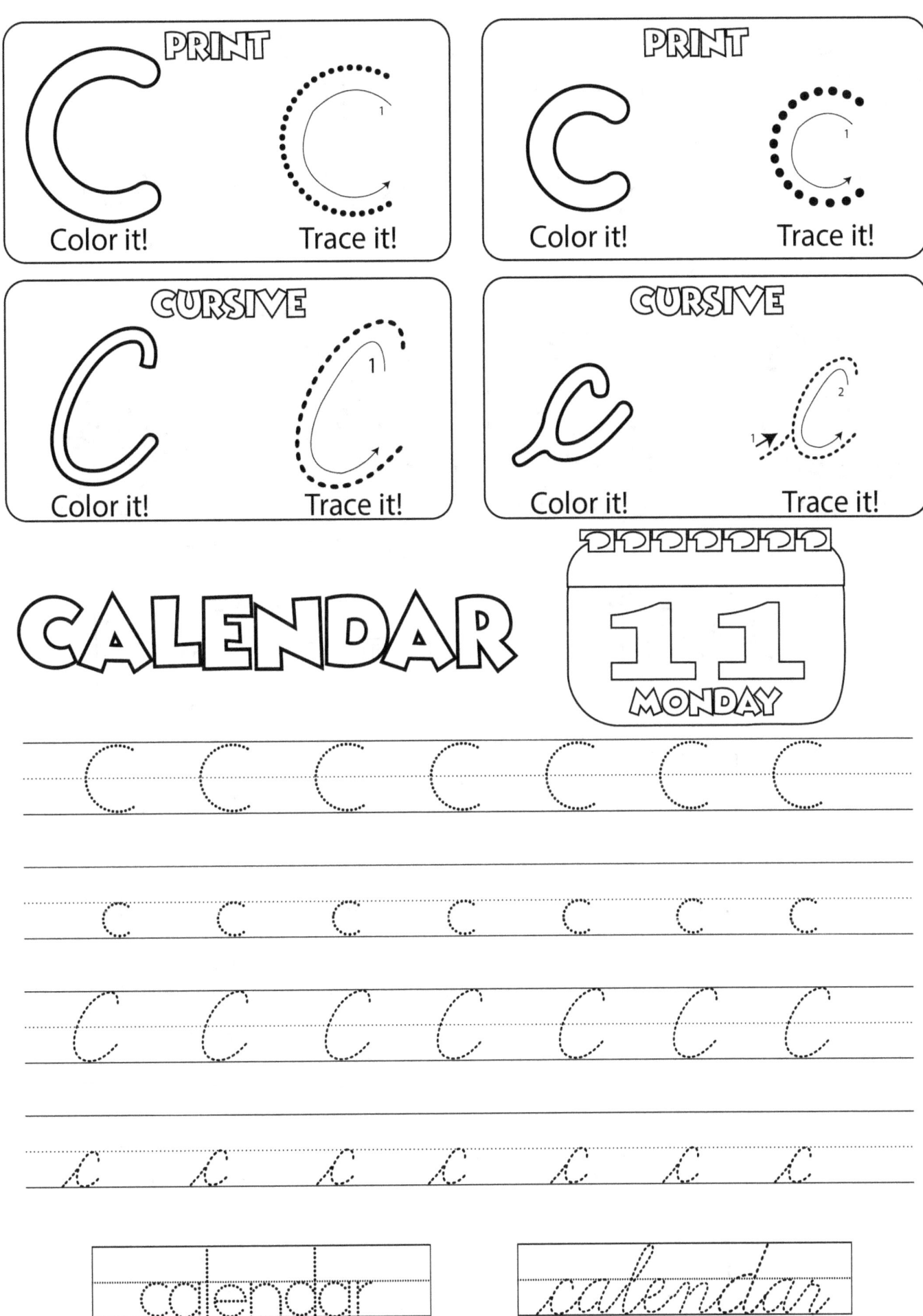

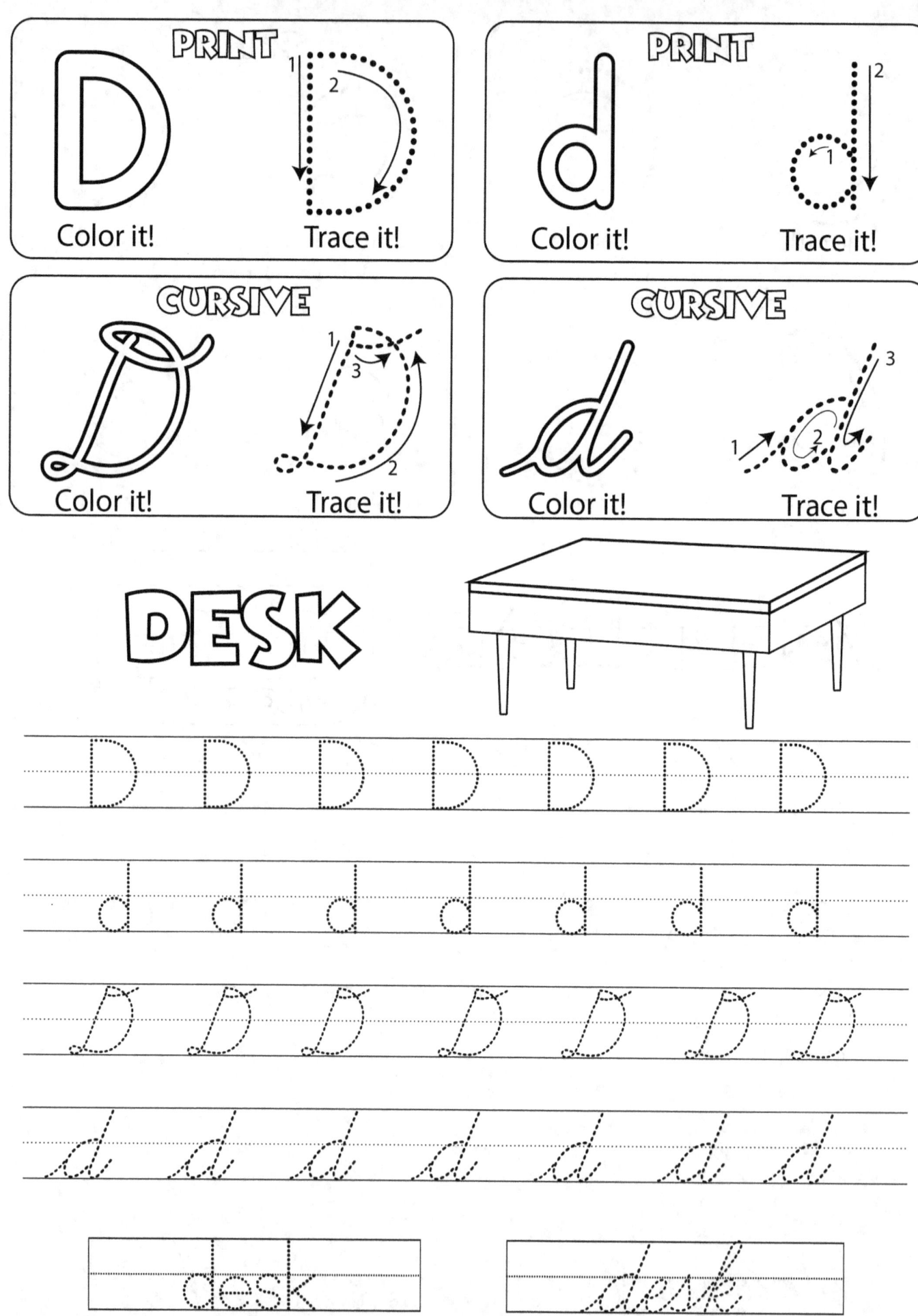

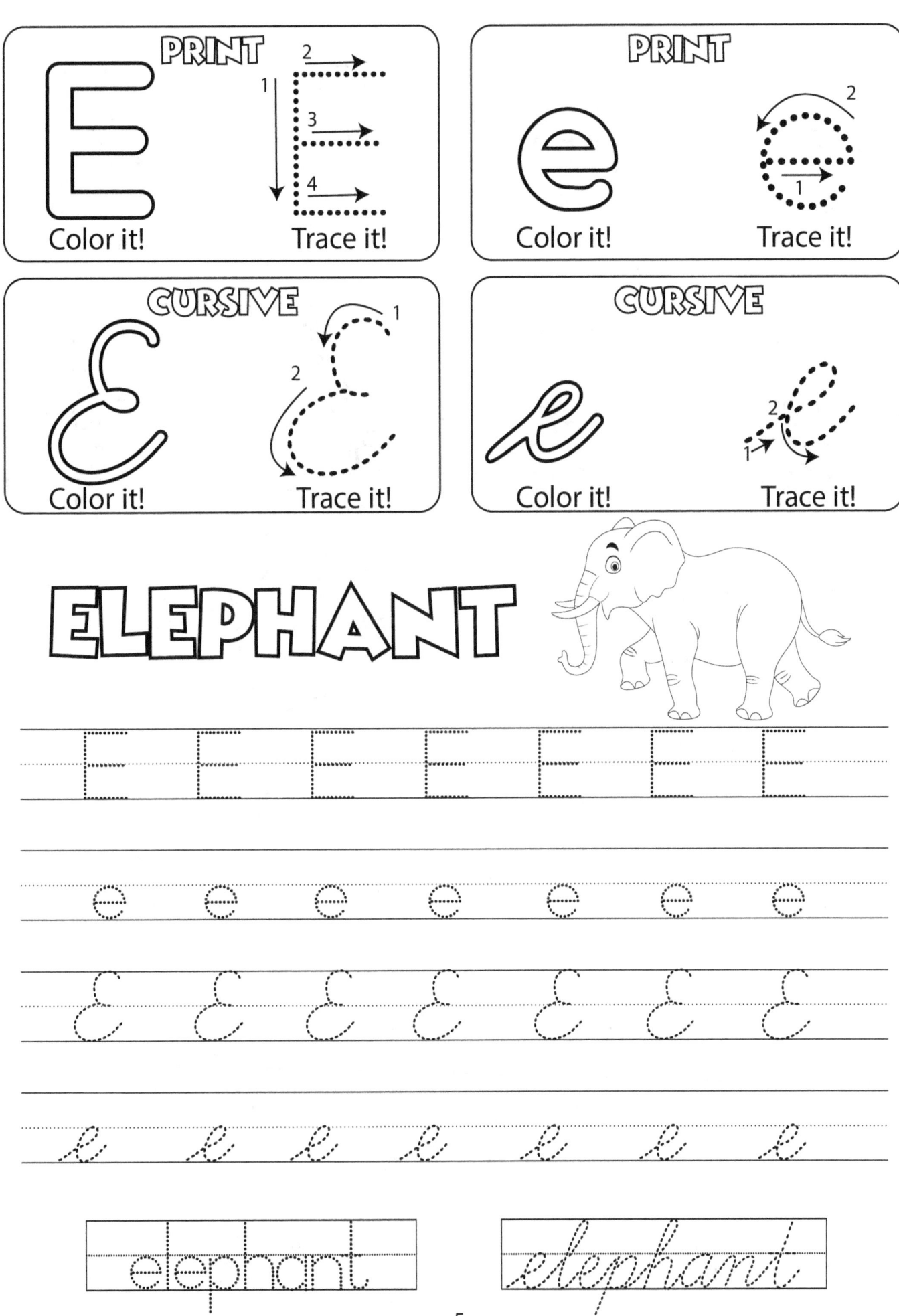

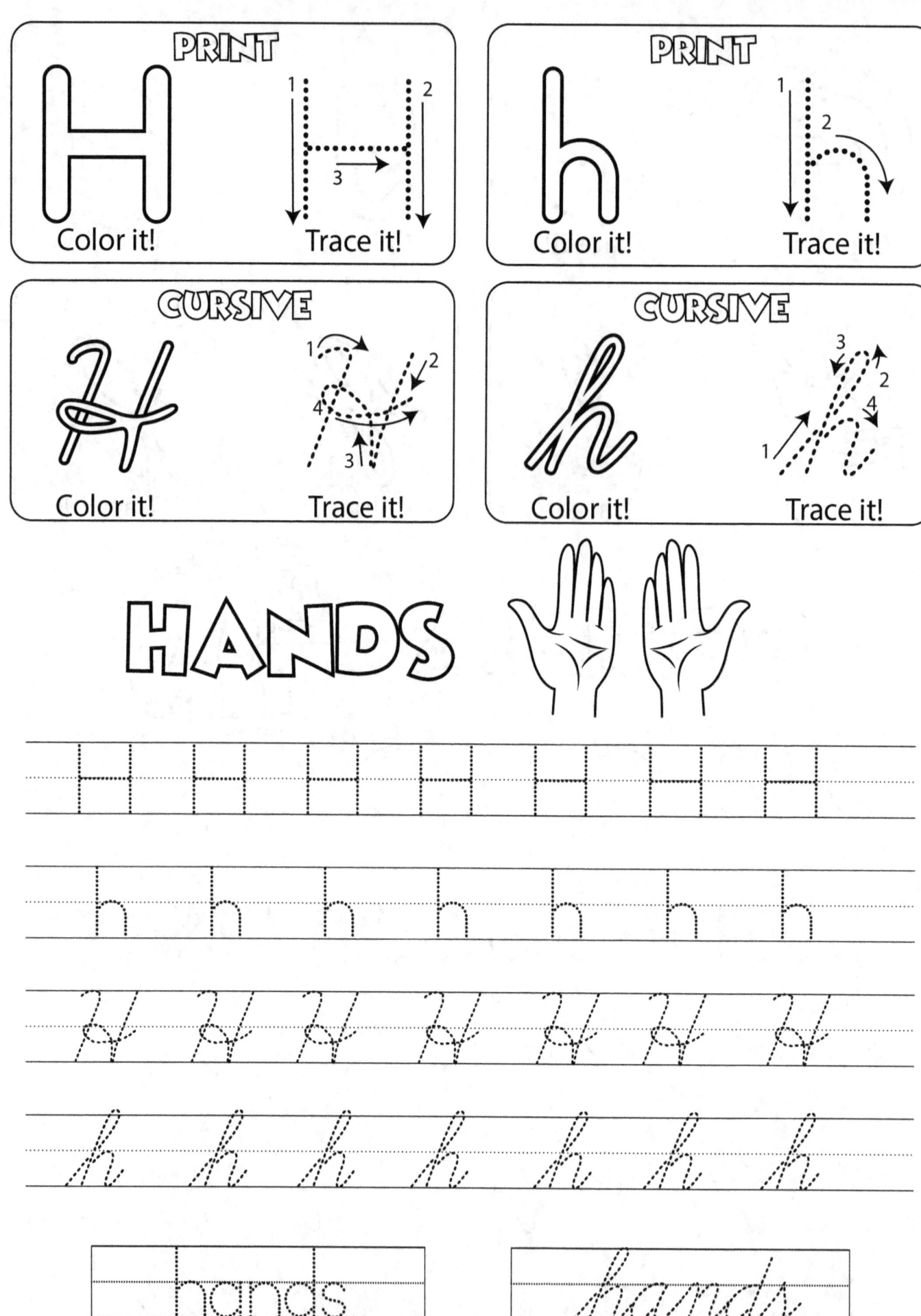

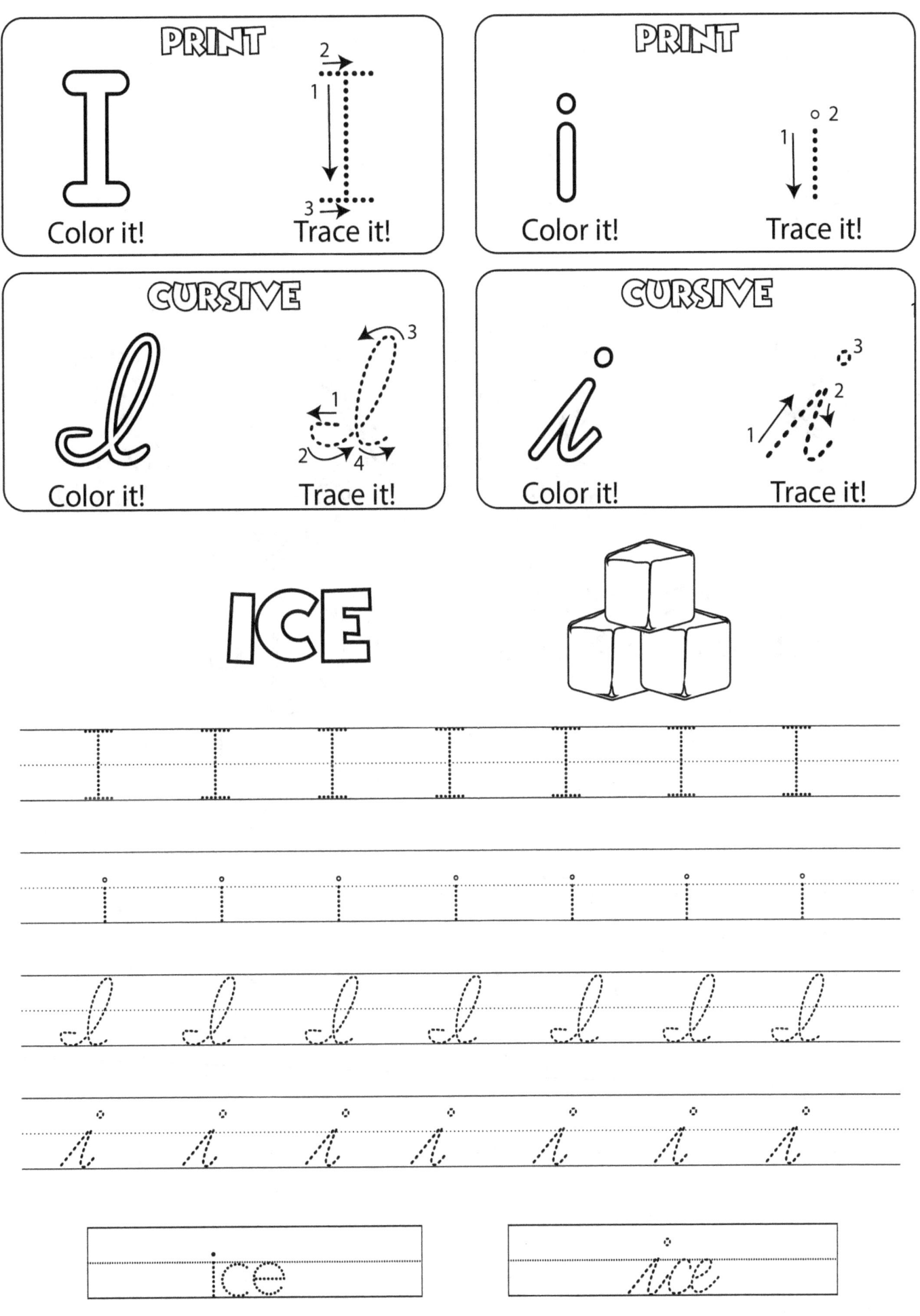

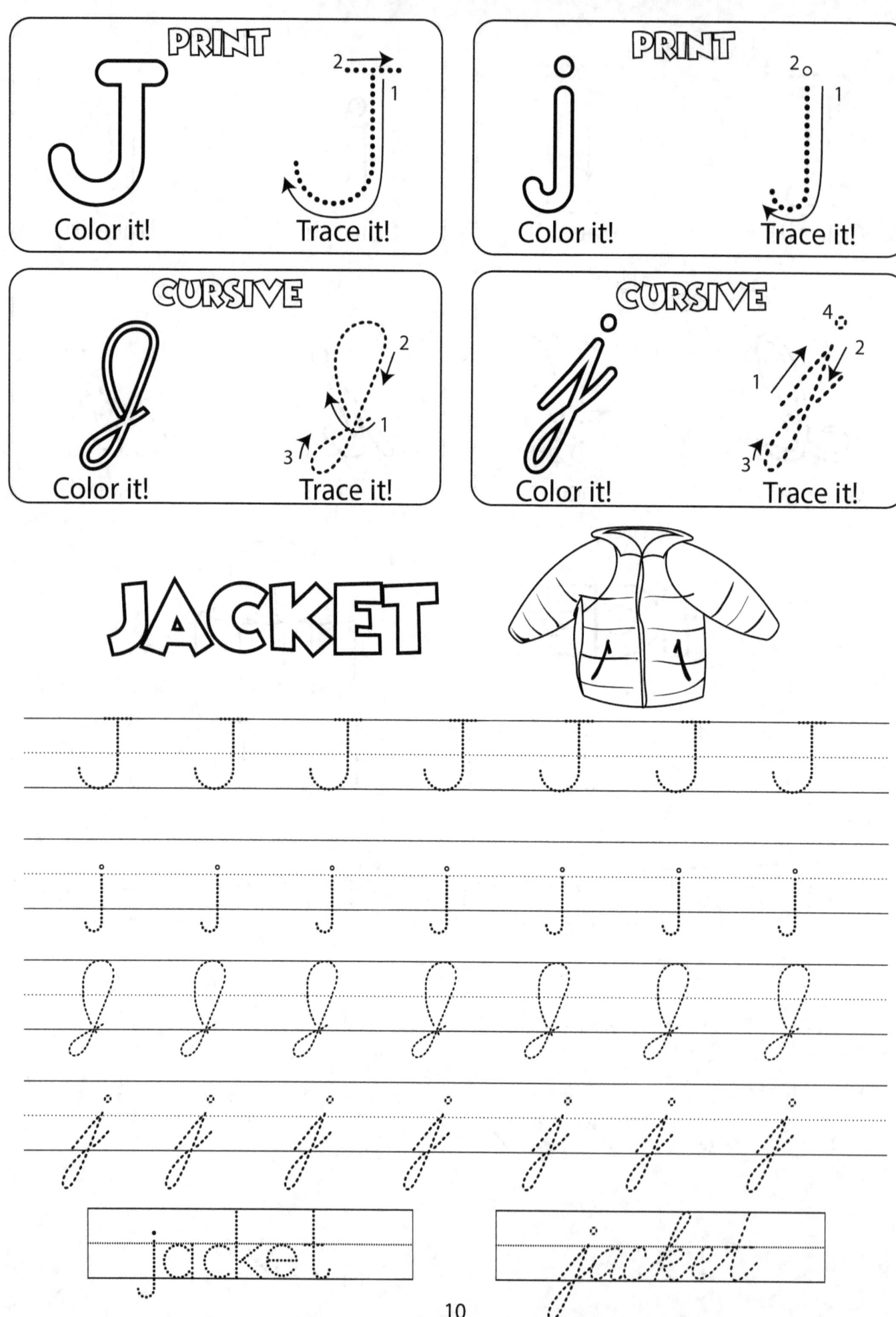

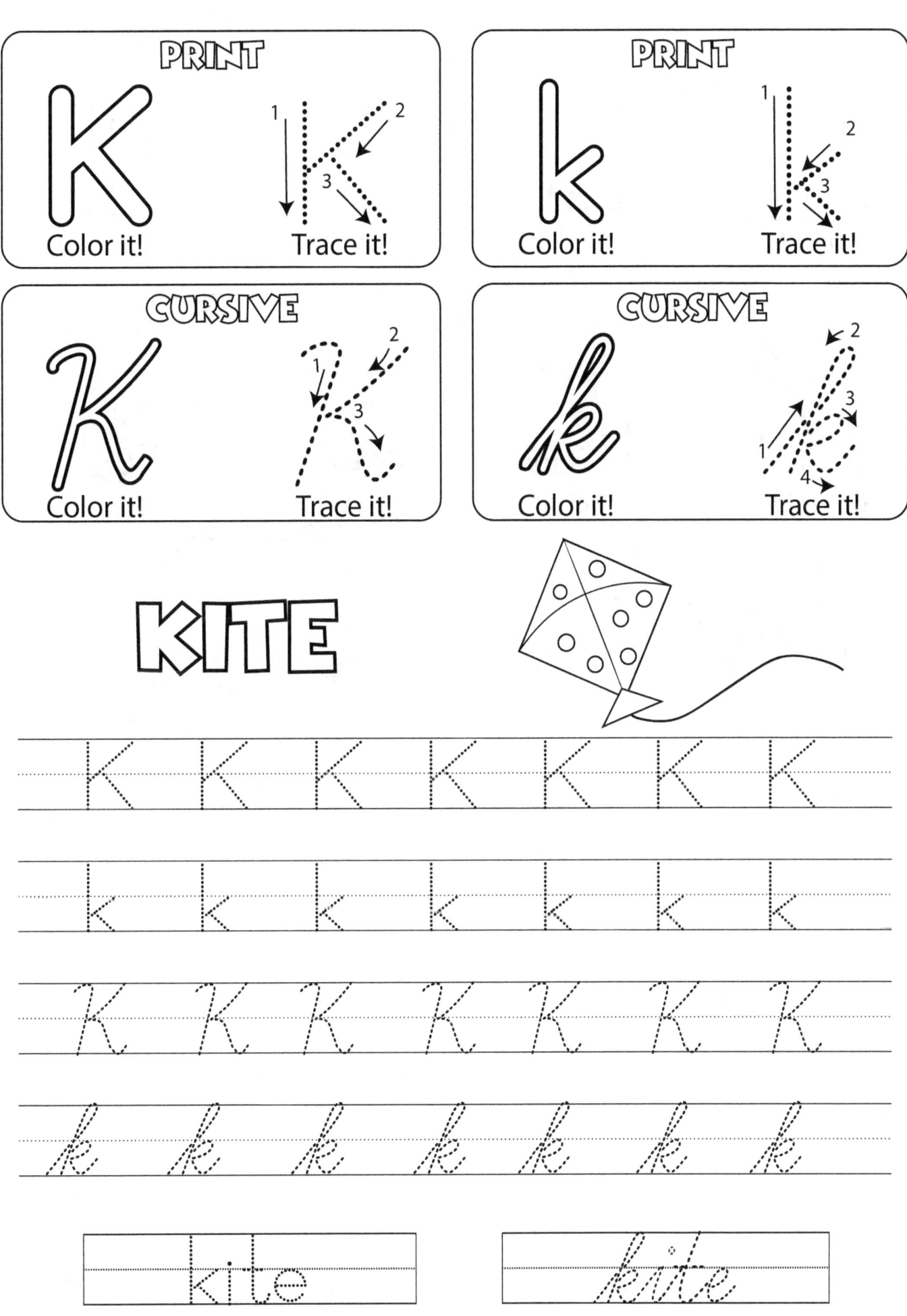

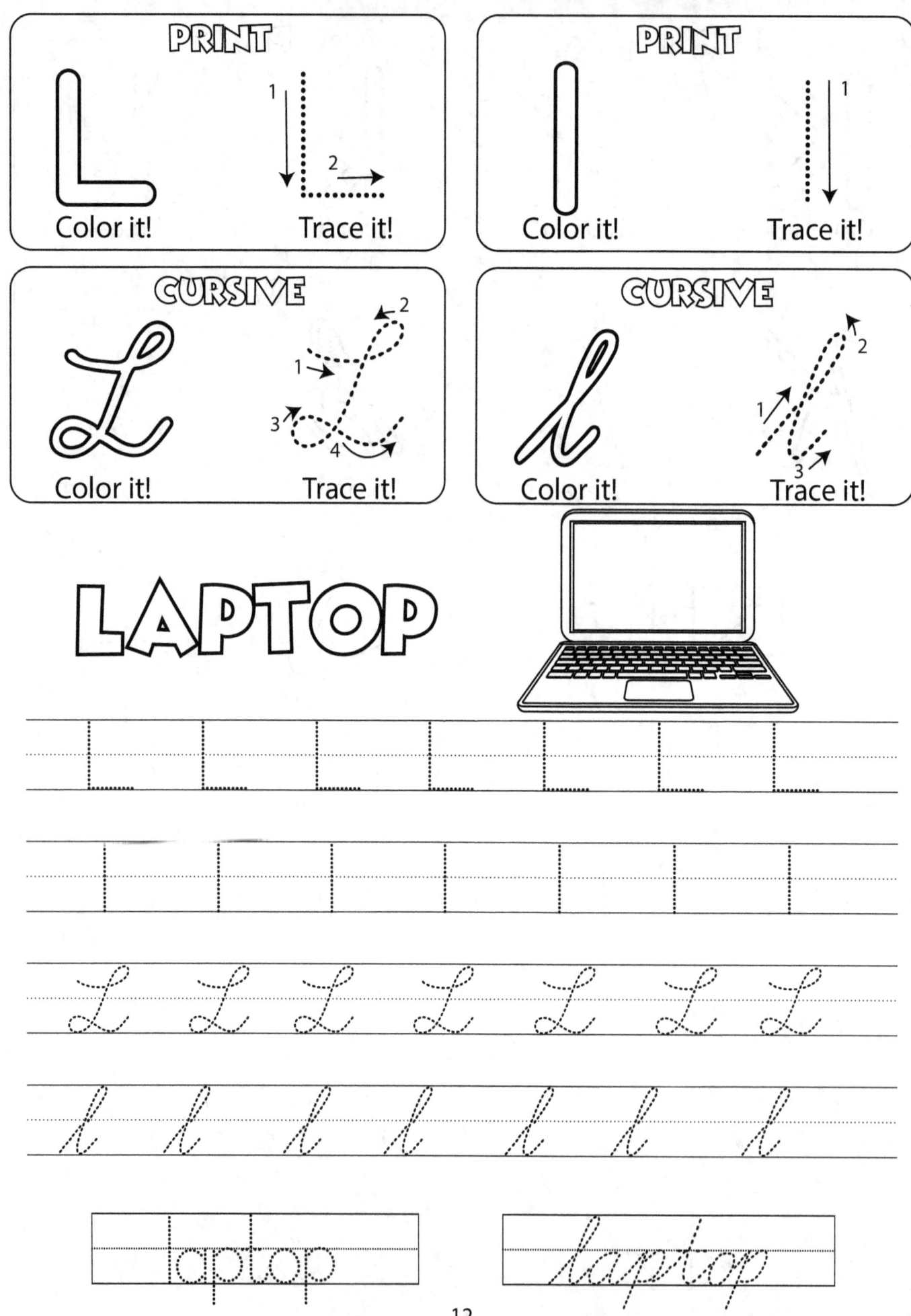

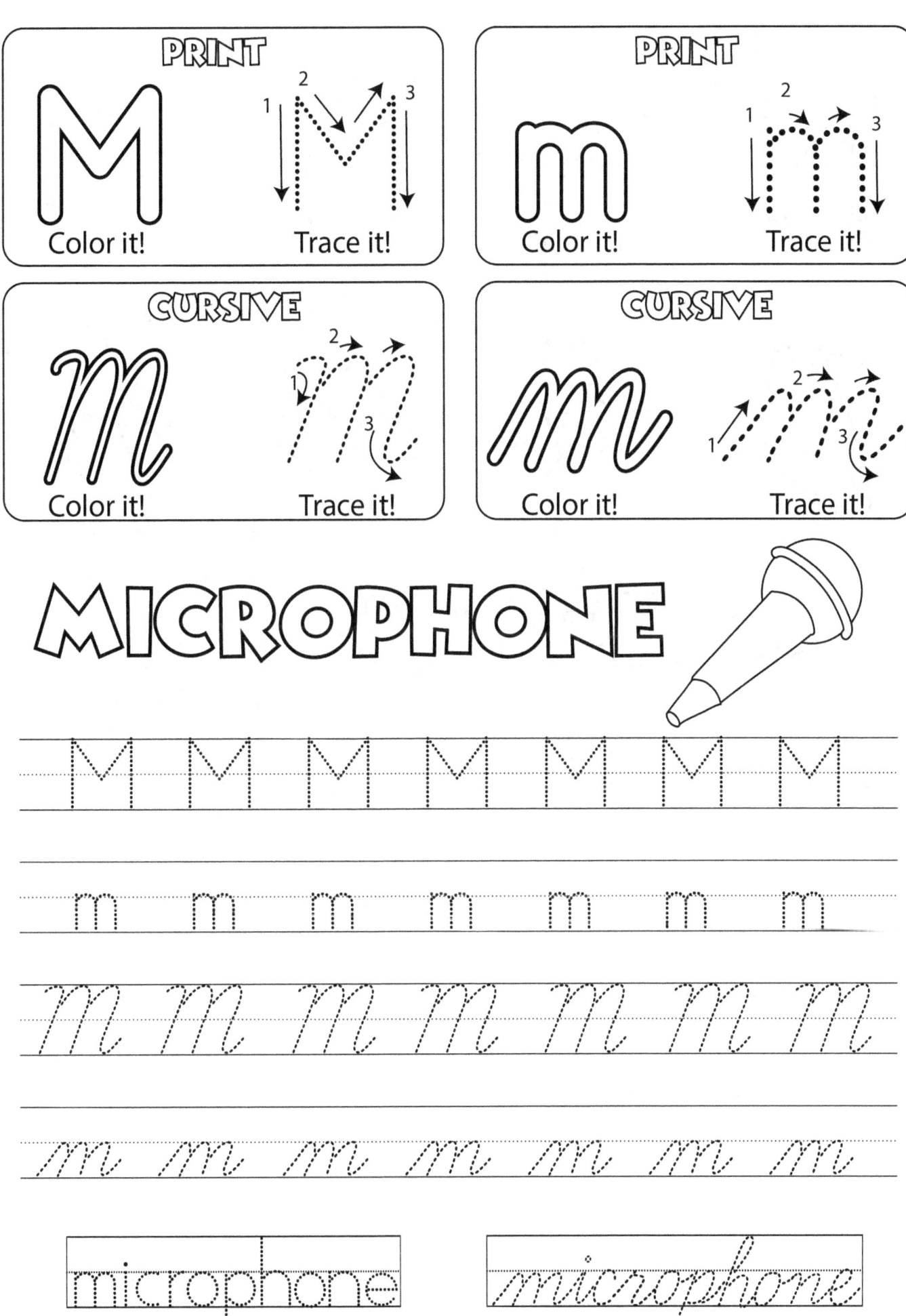

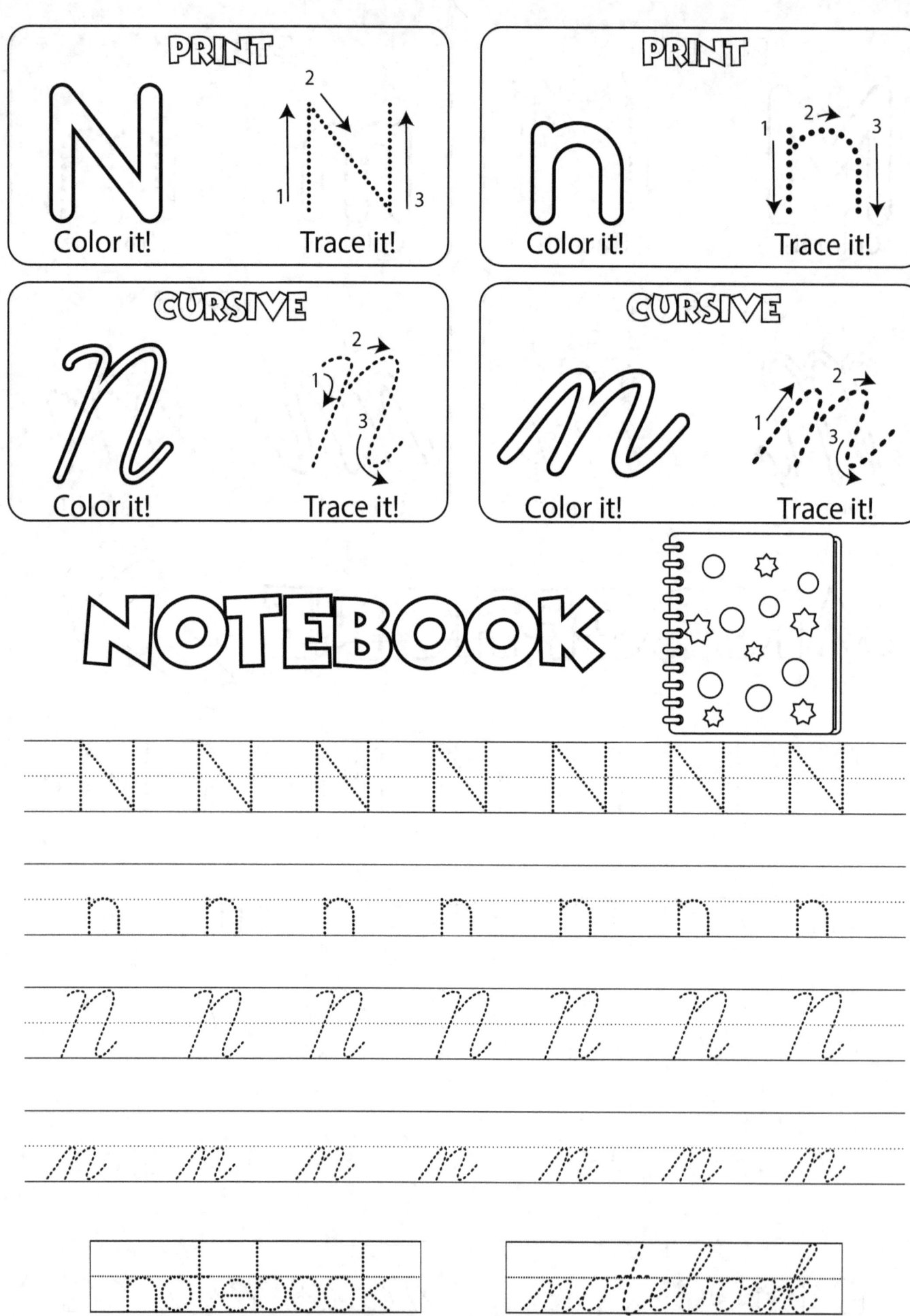

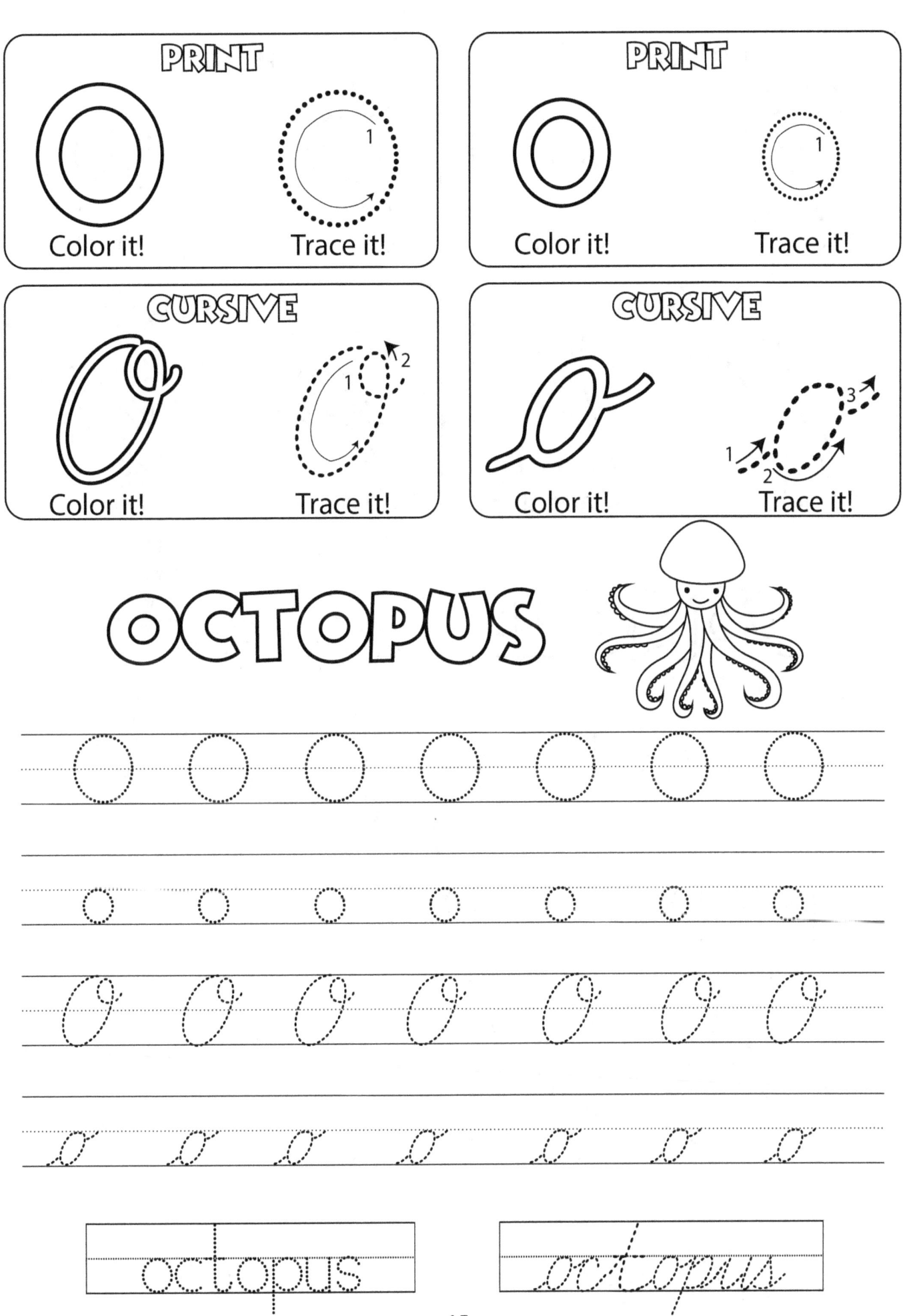

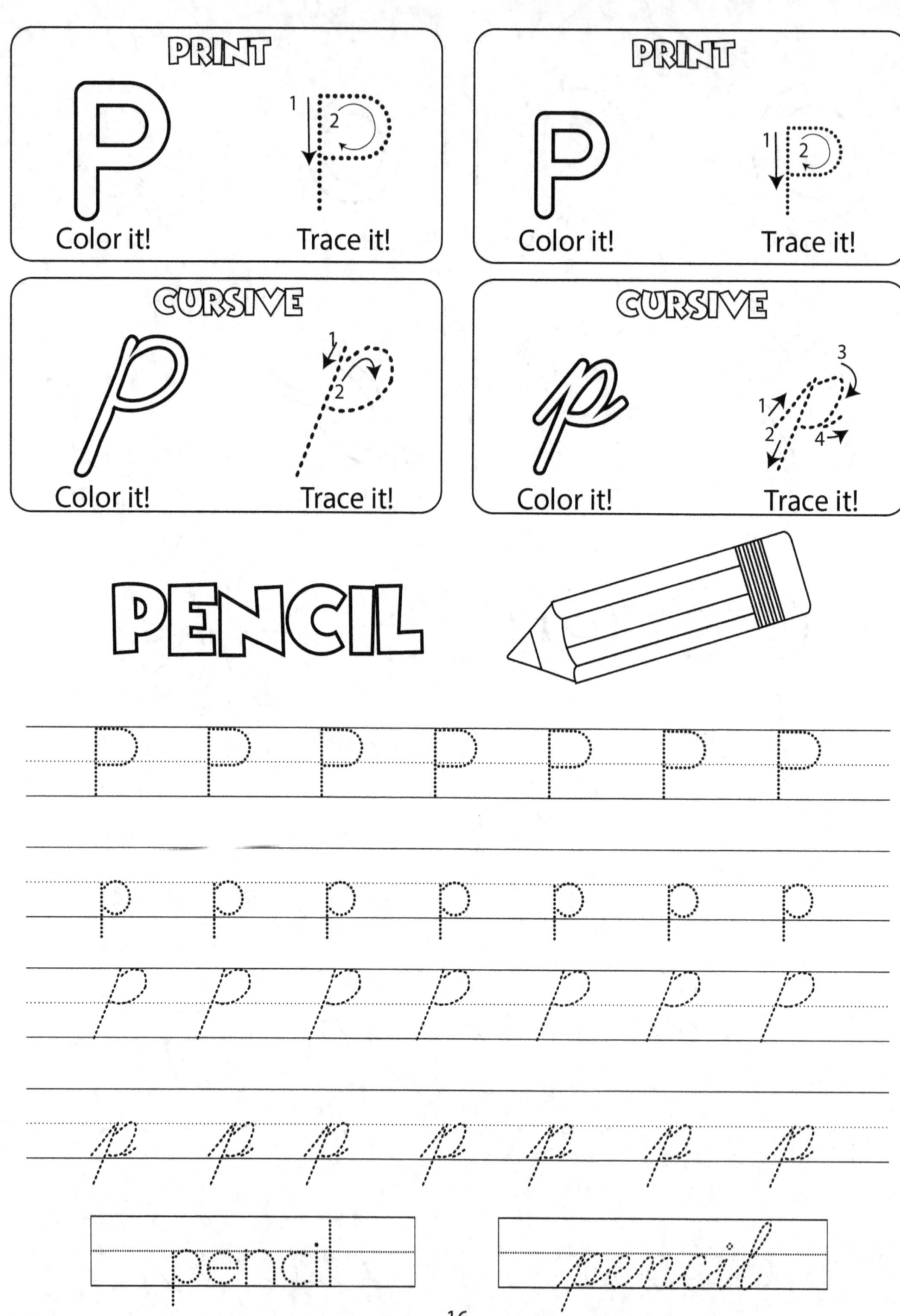

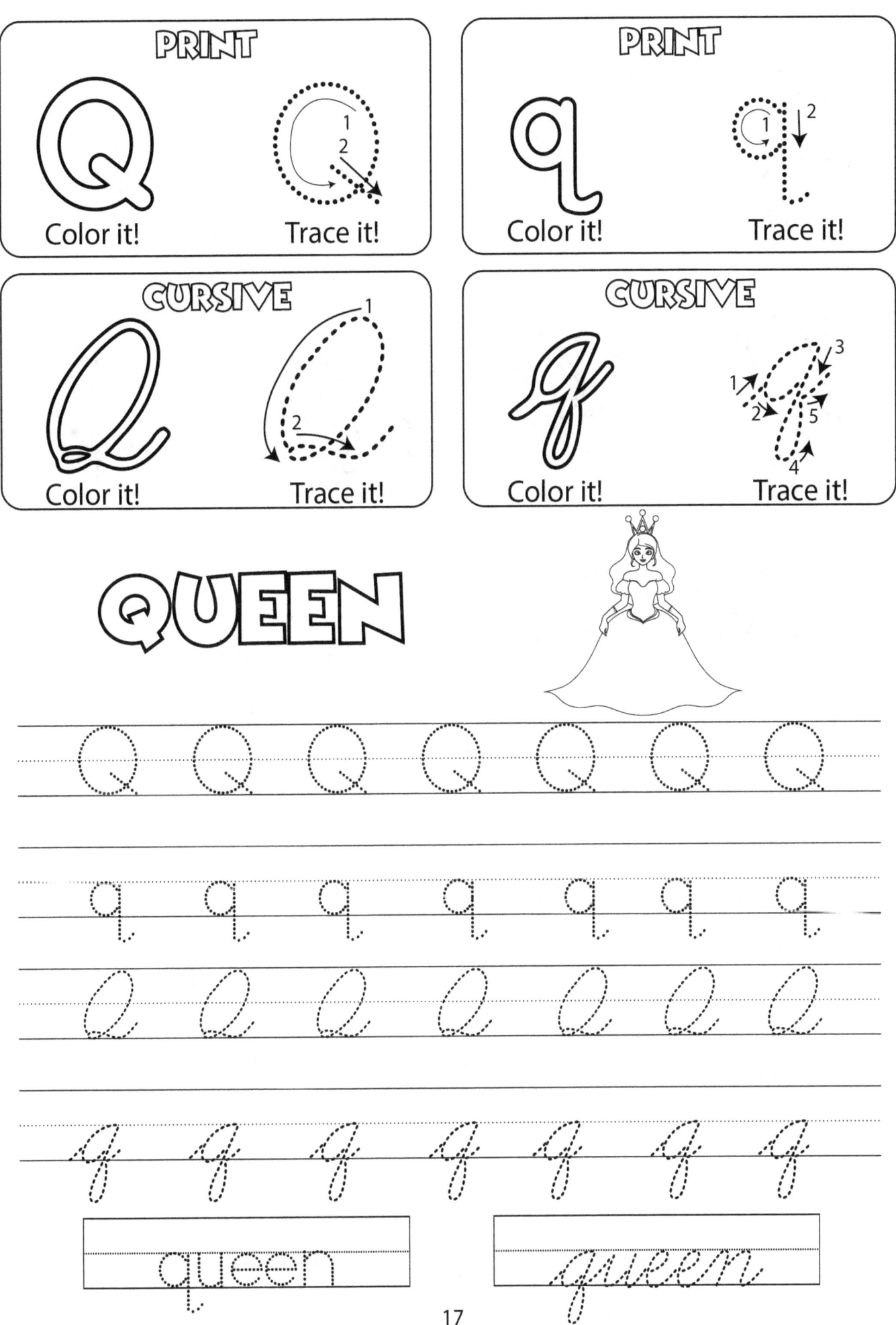

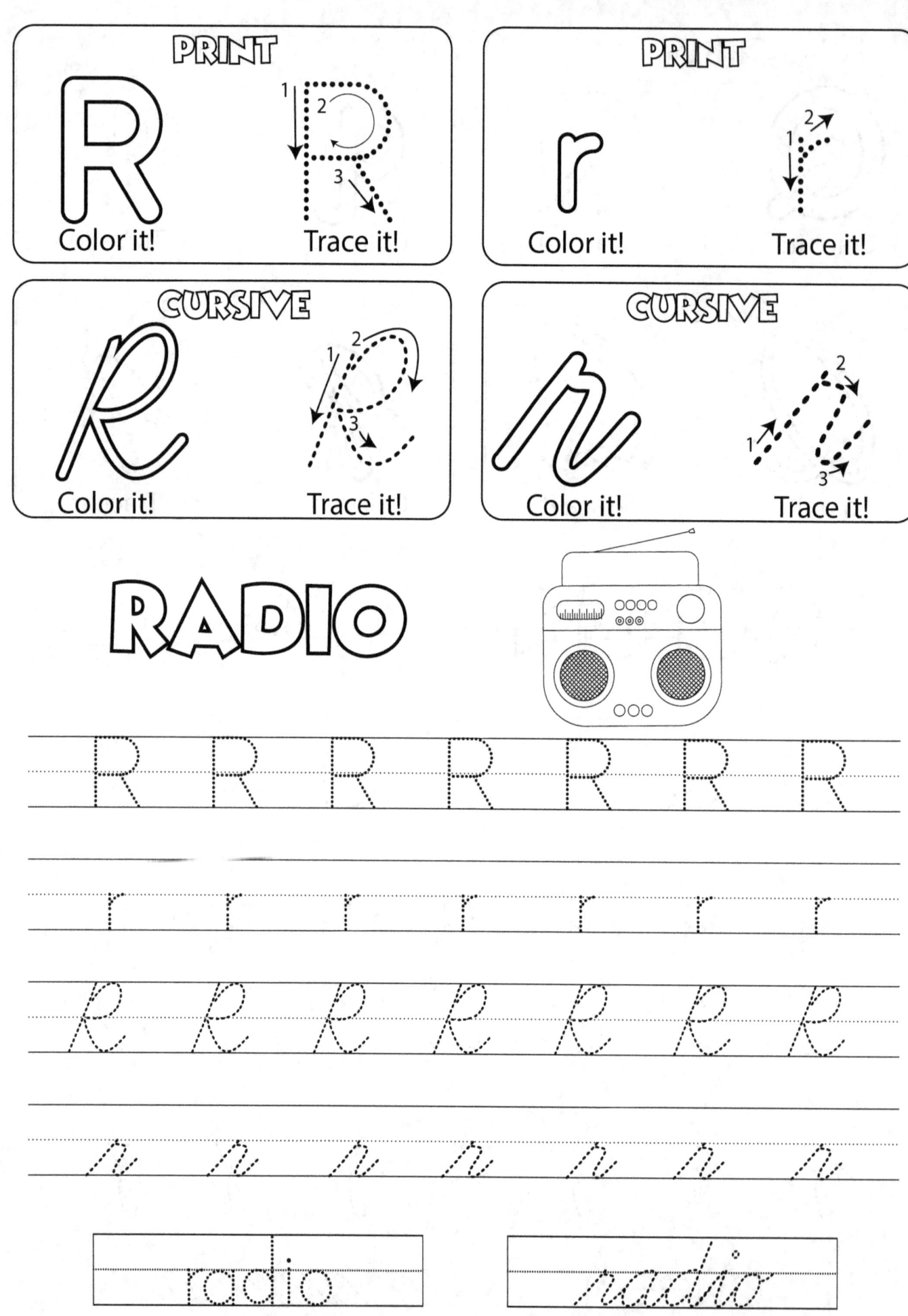

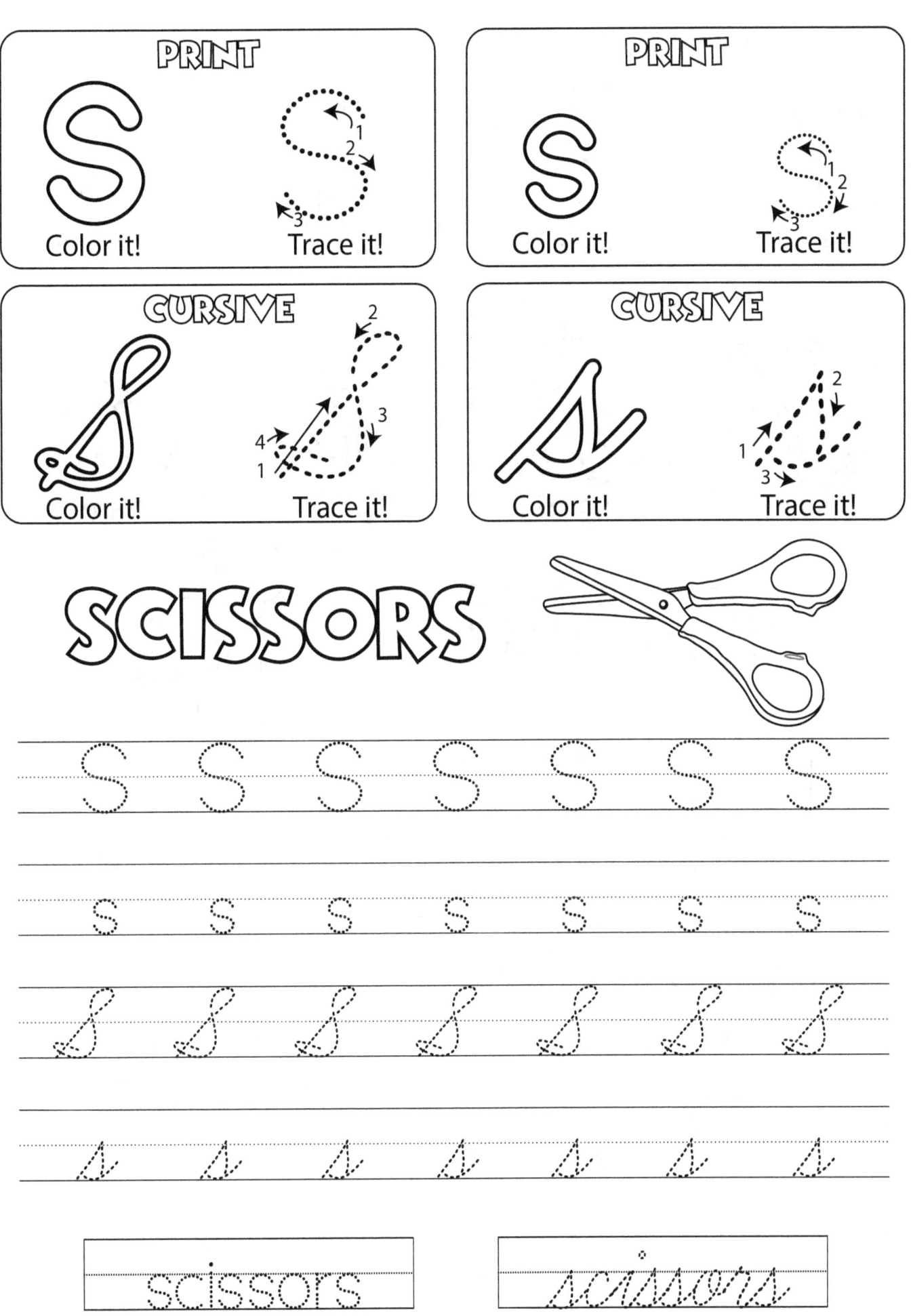

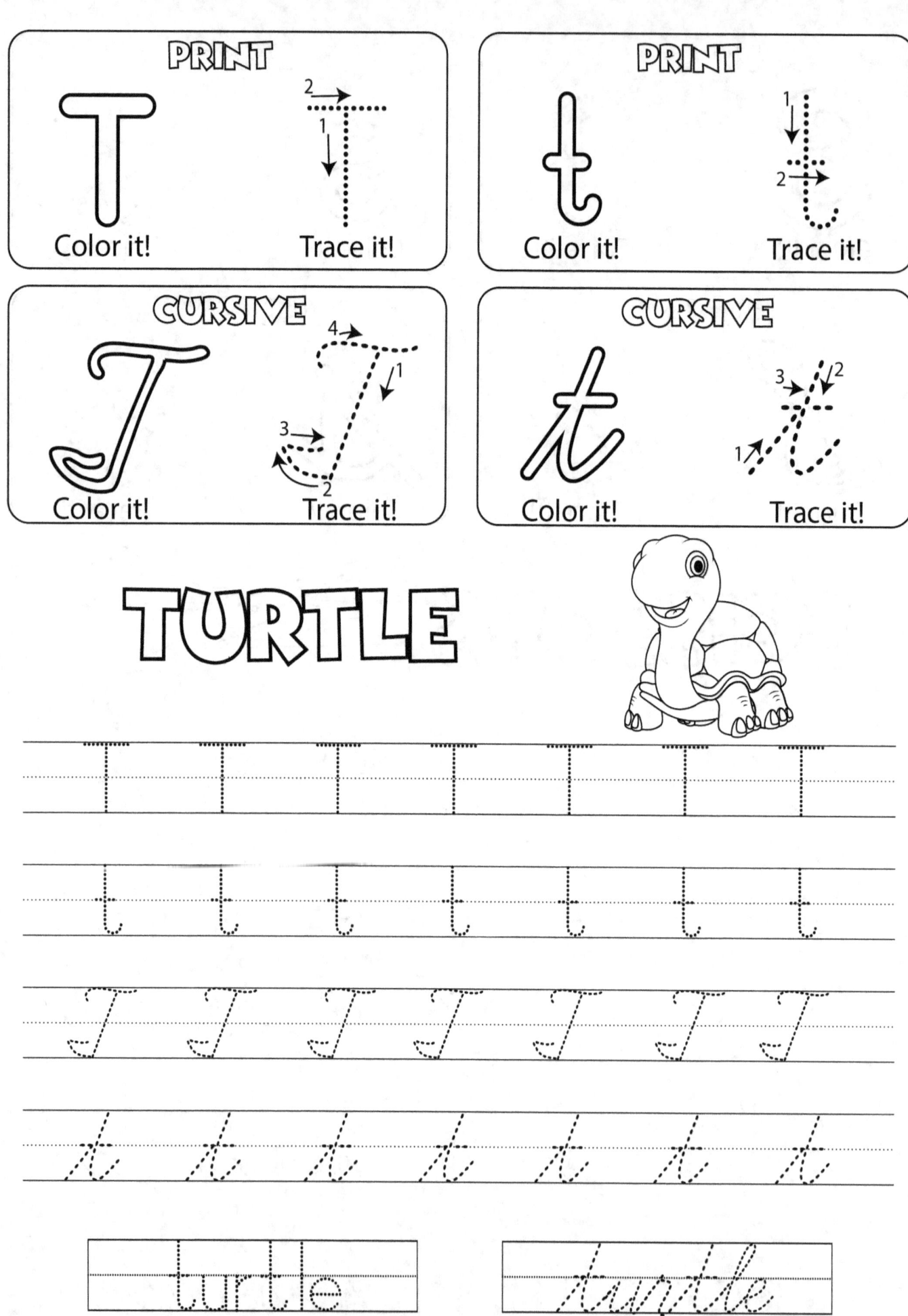

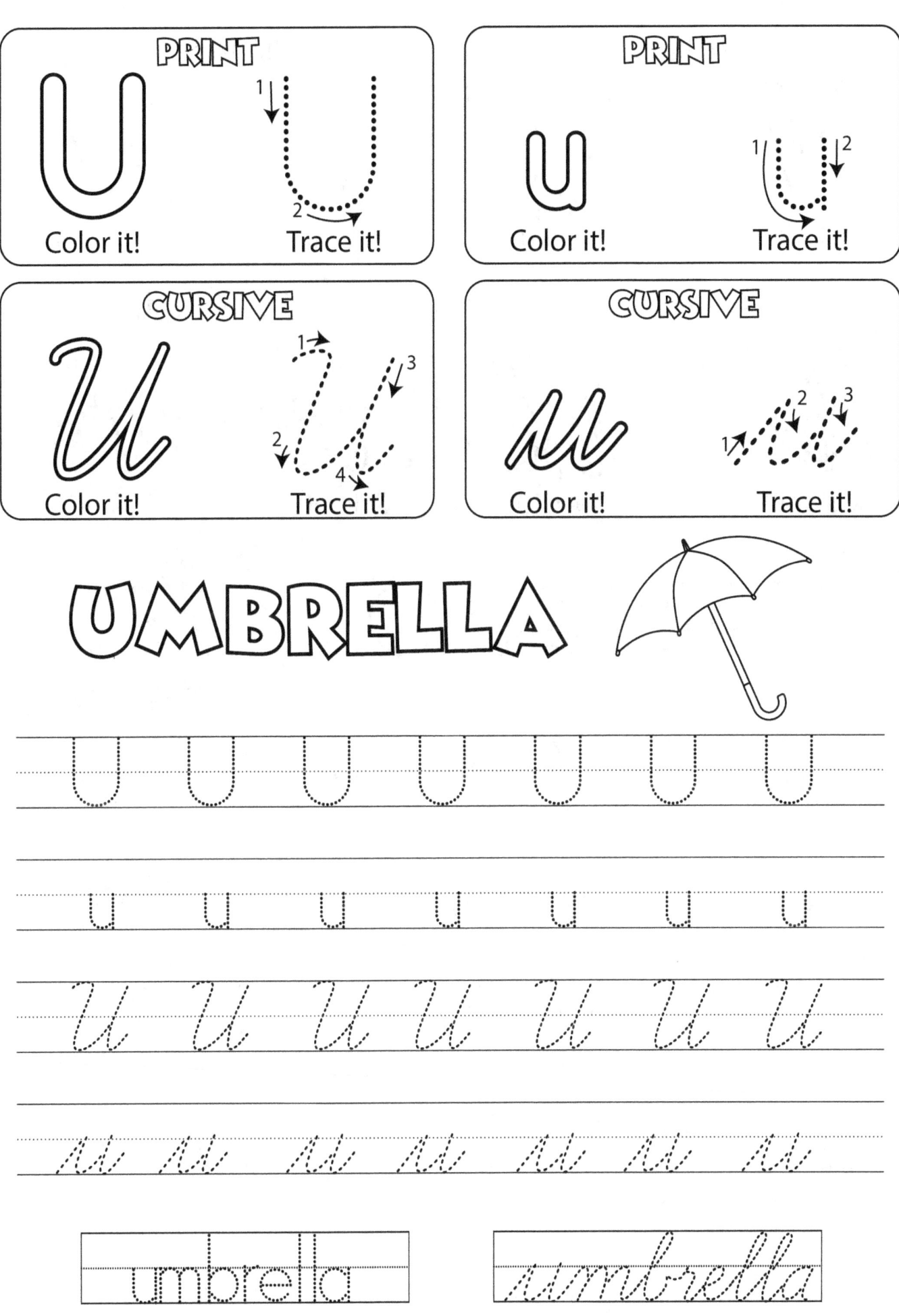

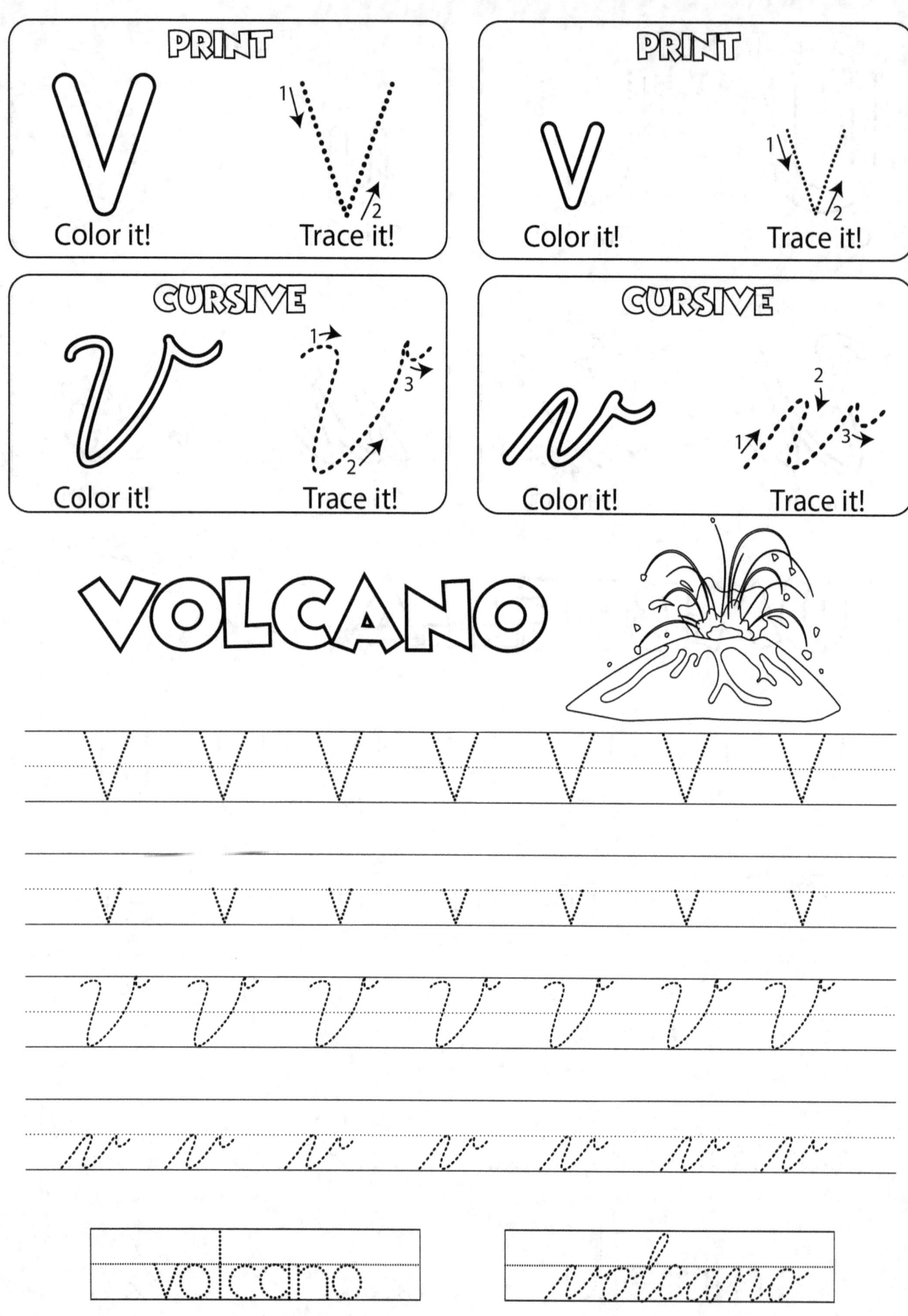

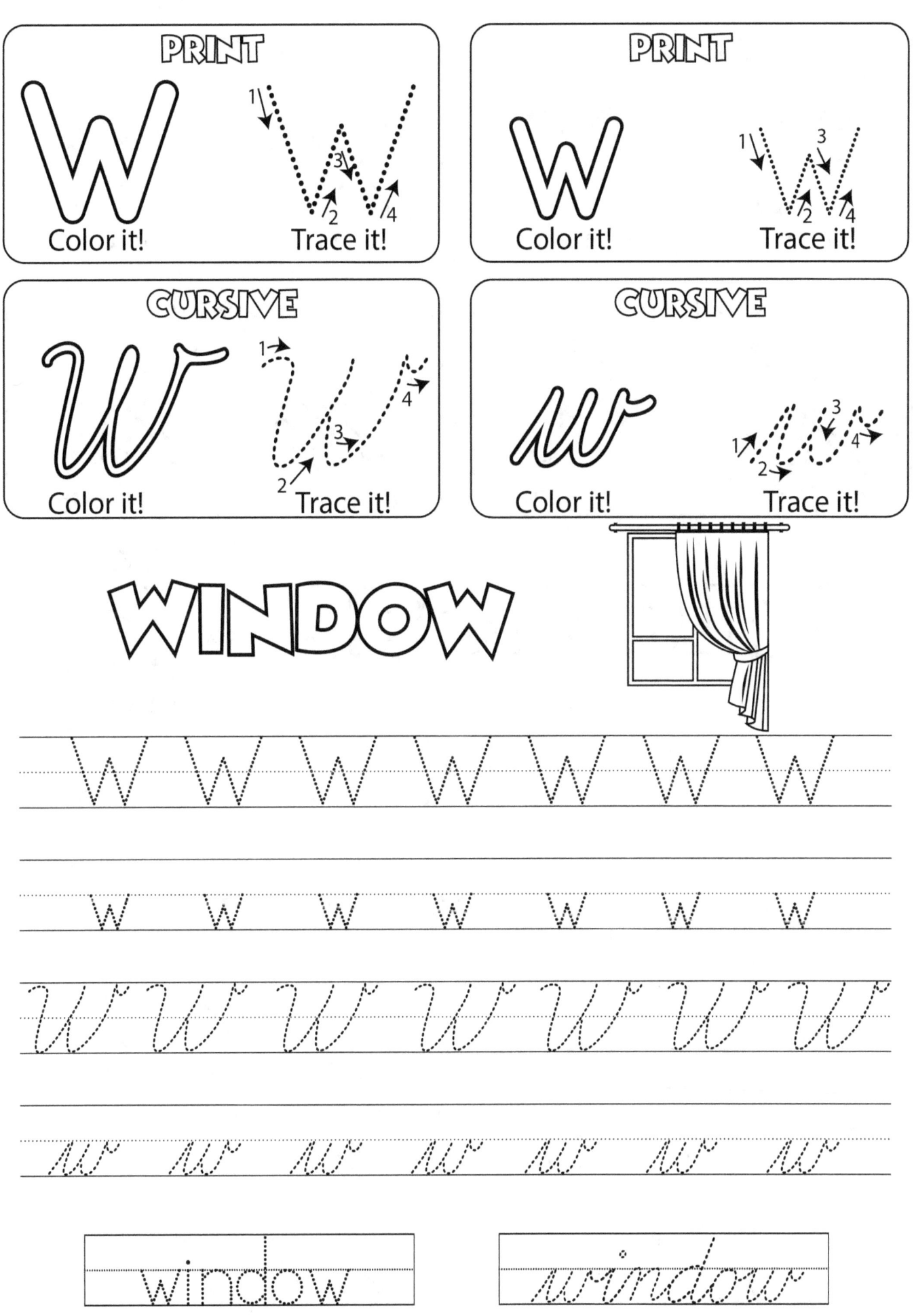

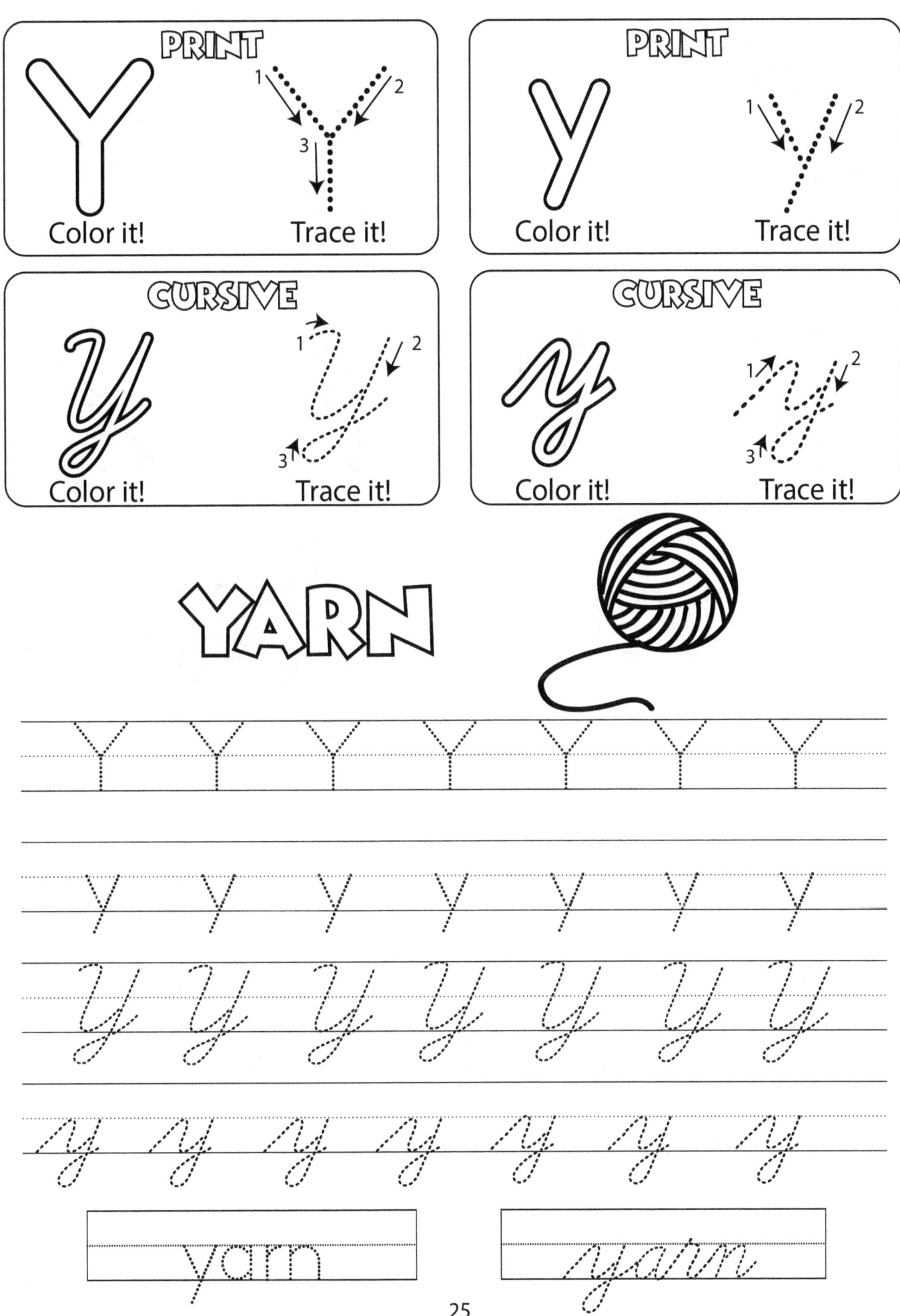

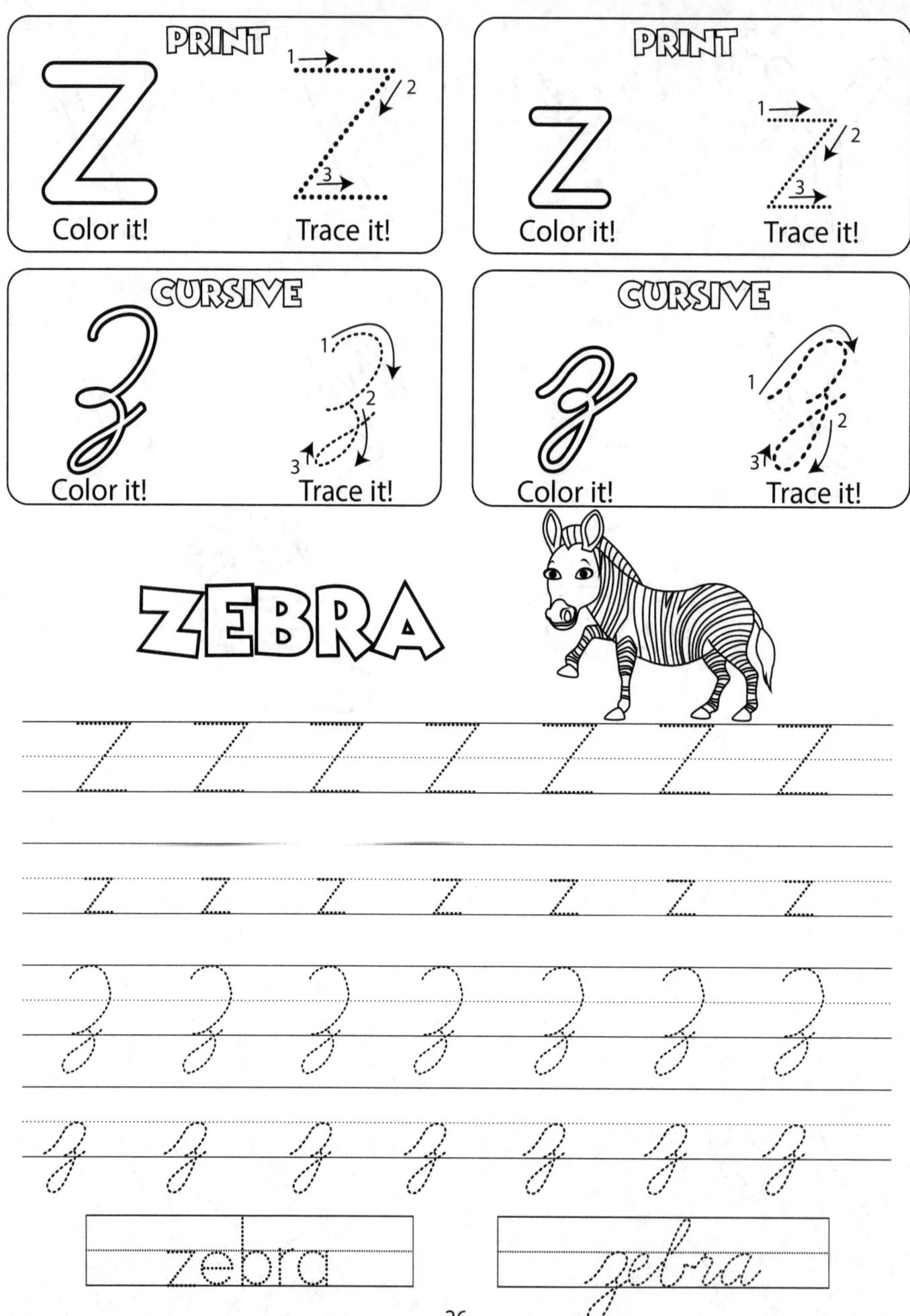

PRACTICE

Aa *Aa*

Bb *Bb*

Cc *Cc*

Dd *Dd*

Ee *Ee*

Ff *Ff*

Gg *Gg*

Hh *Hh*

Ii *Ii*

Jj *Jj*

PRACTICE

Kk *Kk*

Ll *Ll*

Mm *Mm*

Nn *Nn*

Oo *Oo*

Pp *Pp*

Qq *Qq*

Rr *Rr*

Ss *Ss*

Tt *Tt*

PRACTICE

Uu *Uu*

Vv *Vv*

Ww *Ww*

Xx *Xx*

Yy *Yy*

Zz *Zz*

PRACTICE

PRACTICE

airplane — *airplane*

book — *book*

calendar — *calendar*

desk — *desk*

elephant — *elephant*

fish — *fish*

gorilla — *gorilla*

hands — *hands*

ice — *ice*

jacket — *jacket*

PRACTICE

kite — *kite*

laptop — *laptop*

microphone — *microphone*

notebook — *notebook*

octopus — *octopus*

pencil — *pencil*

queen — *queen*

radio — *radio*

scissors — *scissors*

turtle — *turtle*

PRACTICE

umbrella — *umbrella*

volcano — *volcano*

window — *window*

xylophone — *xylophone*

yarn — *yarn*

zebra — *zebra*

PRACTICE

www.ingramcontent.com/pod-product-compliance
Lightning Source LLC
Chambersburg PA
CBHW051215290426
44109CB00021B/2465